"The sheer volume of life messages found within *Surrendered and Untamed* took me by surprise. Beneath the surface of Alex and Sibusiso's seemingly monotonous and colorless trek are layers and hues of heaven for every occasion. From the power of our decisions to our capacity to rise above the impossible, it provides stark reminders of how fearfully and wonderfully made we are. To say that I was humbled by its honesty and stoked by its determination would be an understatement. At times I felt like I was there—part of their epic battle with the most hostile forces on earth. Then it dawned on me. I am!"

— **Dr. Bill Bennot**, lead pastor, His People Johannesburg, South Africa

"It isn't often in the genre of films on faith that you come across something that makes your heart race and adrenaline pump. *Surrendered and Untamed* makes faith look like the vital, muscular, and frankly risky adventure it was always supposed to be. These films will grab the attention of anyone who wants to remember what it is like to come alive to the God we have too often tried to make tame. Not recommended for the fainthearted."

— **Matt Hemsley**, associate pastor, City Church Charlotte

Surrendered *and* Untamed

Participant's Guide

Awaken Your Soul at the Edge of the World

Mark Batterson

with Jason Clark and Joel Clark

BakerBooks

a division of Baker Publishing Group
Grand Rapids, Michigan

© 2011 by Mark Batterson, Jason Clark, and Joel Clark

Published by Baker Books
a division of Baker Publishing Group
P.O. Box 6287, Grand Rapids, MI 49516-6287
www.bakerbooks.com

Printed in the United States of America

Library of Congress Cataloging-in-Publication Data
Batterson, Mark.
    Surrendered and untamed participant's guide : awaken your soul at the edge of the
  world / Mark Batterson with Jason Clark and Joel Clark.
        p.   cm.
    ISBN 978-0-8010-1375-1 (pbk.)
    1. Spirituality. 2. Spiritual life—Christianity. 3. Christian life. I. Clark, Jason. II. Clark,
  Joel. III. Title.
  BV4501.3.B3875 2011
  248.4—dc22   2010042370

Published in association with the literary agency of Alive Communications, Inc., 7680 Goddard Street, Suite 200, Colorado Springs, CO 80920, www.alivecommunications.com.

Permissions for lyrics on page 75.

11   12   13   14   15   16   17   7   6   5   4   3   2   1

Contents

Introduction   7

1. The Promise   13
2. Risk   27
3. The Wilderness   39
4. Destiny   55

The Beginning . . .   71

Introduction

Welcome to the *Surrendered and Untamed* (S&U) participant's guide.

We hope you will enjoy your stay with us. Feel free to doodle on the corners of the pages and make notes in the margins. If you need to remember a phone number, jot it down anywhere, but remember to dog-ear that page. It could be tough to find otherwise. If you want to rip a corner from one of the pages to dispose of your gum, go for it. You won't offend us.

What we are saying is, make yourself at home.

We also hope you will use this book for the purpose we intend it—to capture your journey and propel you further into a *Surrendered and Untamed* walk with God. We hope that over the next several weeks you will be inspired to dream God-sized dreams. And lastly, if we can, we want to make you laugh. A journey without joy hardly seems worth taking . . .

Surrendered and Untamed: The Adventure

In 2006, my (Mark's) good friend and a member of my congregation, filmmaker Joel Clark, signed on to film a documentary about *his* good friend Alex Harris. Alex is a world-renowned explorer. He has been climbing mountains for more than fifteen years. Alex has led more than twenty expeditions to some of the farthest corners of our planet. He has climbed the seven summits—the highest mountains on all seven continents—and has led expeditions up both the north and the south sides of Everest.

Joel and Alex had been friends for years, and when Alex decided to attempt his most daunting and dangerous expedition yet, Joel knew he had to film it. Yet Alex isn't just an insane adventurer who doesn't know when to say no. He is a man who was introduced to Jesus on his first (failed) attempt at Everest. His radical encounter (discussed on the first chapter of the DVD) changed everything about him.

Soon, the simple idea of trekking across Antarctica without any support snowballed into something so much greater than either Alex or Joel could have imagined. Joel went to his brother, Jason Clark, singer, songwriter, and author. Together they began to dream about the idea of taking the message of Jason's most recent album, *Surrendered & Untamed*, and paralleling it with the journey that Alex was about to take. At the time, Alex, Joel, and Jason had no clue that what they were dreaming about would soon become a four-part DVD, a brilliant book by Jason Clark, and this guide.

As their dreams grew, so too did their mammoth task. This was no longer a simple documentary about a man overcoming the most insane and often deadly circumstances that could be found in a place like Antarctica, this was now a series—a beautiful, fierce, and Spirit-breathed message.

That's when Joel called me and asked to have coffee. I had been excited about what Joel was working on without ever truly understanding the depth and beauty of the message. Joel asked me to come on board with *Surrendered and Untamed*, and I was immediately humbled and excited. He asked if I could lend my voice to the project and help define and clarify the message. As I watched an early version of what you are about to see, I felt God in the films. I heard Him saying that this was His heartbeat, and I felt an immediate release to dive in.

As I have come to learn, the Clark brothers never do anything halfway. When I said I would partner with them on this message, I had no idea I would soon find myself on a plane heading for Nevada, spending a lot of time in 100+ degree weather. We filmed in

8

the beautiful and desperately dry desert of Death Valley. The idea was to parallel the fierce environment of Antarctica with the fierce environment of Death Valley. It was not only meant to be beautiful, but when I watch it now, it's as if the desert lends its voice to the message of *Surrendered and Untamed.*

So I want to ask you to open your heart to the journey you are about to embark on. As Alex Harris battles the physical realities of frostbite, crevasse fields, ninety-mile-an-hour winds, and intense loneliness, I want you to think about your own journey. You may not be in Antarctica, but if you look past the physical realities of Alex's journey, you will find that the emotional, psychological, and spiritual journey he is on may closely mirror aspects of your own.

The Promise

Each of us have been given a unique promise from God. In the partner book to this guide, *Surrendered and Untamed: A Field Guide for the Vagabond Believer*, Jason considers what our promise from God looks like:

> I have since heard the promise referred to as *destiny* or *purpose*. That's fine. I believe it's those things. But I like the word *promise* so much more. It implies that I'm not the only one involved in its fulfillment. It suggests that there is more to it than hard work and chance. It hints at relationship. . . .
>
> What does this greater-works promise look like for me? Well, I can't see all of it, but I'm learning that it lives in my heart and can be found in my dreams . . . I also am learning that the only way to see more of it, to engage it, is to develop a believing heart.[1]

I love how Jason describes the search for and the discovery of our promise. It's found in our dreams, the ones that are both exciting and also risky. It's about love, trust, and goodness. It's about believ-

---

1. Jason Clark, *Surrendered and Untamed: A Field Guide for the Vagabond Believer* (Grand Rapids: Baker, 2011), 20, 24.

ing in a God who always loves, is always trustworthy, and is always good. It's about faith.

There is something beautiful about witnessing someone else's faith that inspires faith in us. This journey you are about to watch, the journey you are on, is a faith journey. We are created to dream with God and then step out in faith. And while the journey God has for us is risky, it is always worth it. Always.

How It Works

We've written this guide to be used in a group context. That doesn't mean individuals can't get something out of it, but the group context is our operating assumption throughout the book.

Icebreaker

Each group time will begin with an icebreaker (seemed fitting since most of this film takes place on ice!). These are meant to be fun activities that will get everyone out of "work mode" and into the "let's relate some and laugh more" mode. Some of the meditations and questions are for the group to discuss, while others are more private. All are meant to start you dreaming and believing.

Ponderings

You will want to fill out this section before viewing the film. This is the place where we begin to prepare our hearts.

DVD

Enjoy.

Group Discussion

The group discussion is a time to go a little deeper. We are created for community, first with the Father, Son, and Holy Spirit, and then with each other. The Bible tells us that iron sharpens iron, and we hope that these group discussions can be a place where this happens.

Meditation

This section is for you and God. If you would rather take the guide home, or to the park, or the local ice cream shop, that's fine. Write down the revelations God gives you regarding your journey with Him.

Links for the Week

This *Surrendered and Untamed* guide is much more than the few pages you hold in your hand. This book is filled with multiple web links that will take you deep into the world of S&U each week. Joel and Jason have set up this website:

www.surrenderedanduntamed.com

The website contains over sixty quality films that are as entertaining as they are meaningful. These films will give you a deeper, more intimate look into Alex Harris's expedition to the South Pole. For example, if you want to see what it takes to land a massive Russian Ilyushin on a natural ice runway in Antarctica during high winds, go to this address:

www.surrenderedanduntamed.com/landing

If you don't want to see it—that's OK, no pressure. It's not like it's amazing or anything . . .

But it *is* amazing *and* you will want to remember this link, trust me.

S&U Experiences

Each chapter offers three "S&U Experiences" that are totally optional. These are placed at the end of each chapter, to be read between group meetings.

The *first* experience every week will be an excerpt from the book *Surrendered and Untamed: A Field Guide for the Vagabond Be-*

11

liever written by Jason. The book is not based on Alex's trek to the South Pole, like this guide is. However, the *Surrendered and Untamed* journey is not just about a trip taken by a really amazing explorer, it's about a lifestyle. We all have promises from God, and the book releases us to both discover and fully embrace them. If anything you watch in the DVD or read in this guide encourages you, I'd like to suggest you pick up a copy of the book if you haven't already. I truly believe it will speak to you on a much deeper and more intimate level about living a surrendered and untamed life.

The *second* experience will have a link to a song from the album *Surrendered & Untamed*. As I said in the introduction, this entire series was birthed when Jason Clark recorded this album. The guide you hold in your hands, the DVD, and the book take the message of S&U to a deeper level. Yet the album holds the heartbeat of the *Surrendered and Untamed* journey. Throughout this guide, we'll use lyrics from the album that will help the journey resonate within you.

The *third* experience will contain insights into Alex's trip, from the practical ("How do you fight frostbite in −30 degree weather?") to the more spiritual ("How do you keep believing in what God said when everything seems to be against you?"). This experience includes links to extra footage from the film.

1

The Promise

We know we are on track when the very sight of the thing that is in our heart—the promise—fills us with both intimidating fear but also the most unbelievable excitement.

—Alex

 Icebreaker

In five minutes or less (per person), go around the room and introduce yourself. Don't simply say your name and where you are from, tell a little bit of your story. What makes you, you? What passions and dreams do you have that set you apart from anyone else? If you've known each other for a while, or even if you haven't, try to tell the group something most people don't know about you.

13

Ponderings

Take a moment to read through the section below and write your answer to the question.

I (Jason) have three kids. They are dreamers—all kids are dreamers. They want to go to space, fight dragons, live in castles, and ride on flying ponies up to swimming pools in the clouds. They want to have superpowers and eat ice cream in bed. Many of their dreams are simply the wonderful fantasies of children. However, I believe that their promises from God are hidden in their dreams.

Jesus said,

> Unless you change and become like little children, you will never enter the kingdom of heaven. (Matt. 18:3)

Children can often tell you exactly what they want to do or be; they can easily define those things that make them "come alive." As we grow up, we can lose the ability to dream like when we were kids. Life is crazy, and it almost seems as if, in order to "make it," we have to put away the "childish" dreaming. I believe that this is one of the reasons Jesus tells us to become like children. He wants us to dream wild dreams again.

When you were a kid, what did you dream about? What did you hope you might become? Think of the craziest dreams you had! They don't have to be possible. If you wanted to walk on the moon (that was made of cheese, of course), so be it! Write it down in the space provided below.

 DVD

Now it's time for the big moment. Put in the DVD, find the first chapter titled "The Promise," and press Play.

We'll follow South African explorer Alex Harris on a 65-day, 692-mile unsupported trek across Antarctica. I believe we're going to learn some lessons that will help us live a truly surrendered and untamed life.

—Mark

My promise is to get to these places alive and to come back with the stories and to tell people what the journey was like. And hopefully inspire the promise in others to awaken.

—Alex

When you get Christ, you get all of the promises—it's a package deal. But the key is surrender. You have to surrender your life to Jesus Christ.

—Mark

The size of the obstacle before you is in direct proportion to the greatness that God is thrusting upon you.

—Graham Cooke

15

 Group Discussion

Take some time to discuss the video with the group.

1. What are your first impressions of Alex's comments that this trek is God's promise being fulfilled in his life?

2. What stood out to you in light of your journey? Was there anything that caused you to think more outside the box regarding God's promises for our lives?

3. Was there anything that Alex or Mark said that you connected with? Why?

4. I (Mark) referred to *that deep place within your soul that longs for spiritual adventure.* What does the term "spiritual adventure" mean to you? When have you experienced it?

5. Is there an adventure that calls to you, something that maybe you often dream of but haven't actually pursued? This is a great place to share it.

 Meditation

Take 5–10 minutes to write your answers to the questions below. When everyone is done, go around the group one last time and explain one of your answers below.

1. Earlier you wrote about your childhood dreams. Now write some of the dreams you still have. They will most likely look different, they may not be as fanciful, and they may not be burning desires, but they should stir your heart with excitement. It could be as simple as "I have always dreamed of going to the Grand Canyon" or "traveling to Africa." Or it may be more of a life goal: "I have always dreamed of working with an orphanage in China." Or it could be more structured—like learning a skill set such as carpentry or graphic design. Whatever it is, it should stir your heart with excitement. Write it here:

2. In the film, Alex says something that makes me (Mark) smile every time I hear it. He was talking about the first time he saw Everest with his own eyes. He said, "*It took my breath away— but I'm not going to lie to you that I didn't feel fear in that*

17

moment. I trembled. . . . We know we are on track when the very sight of the thing that is in our heart—the promise—fills us with both intimidating fear but also the most unbelievable excitement."

Is there anything that you can think of that causes you to react this way? What causes you to fear and yet at the same time holds "unbelievable excitement"? You may need to spend a little time thinking through this one. It may be similar to the answer above, or it may be completely different. It could be as simple as the idea of "skydiving" or as courageous as "owning my own business." Don't worry, there is no wrong or right answer here.

3. Alex Harris is on an expedition to the South Pole. He is there because he is laying hold of his promise. He is there because he first dreamed it. He is there because, at least in part, this is what God created him to do. Alex once told me that the times and places where he "most tangibly feels the presence of God" are when he is on a mountain or exploring the most remote reaches of our planet.

Is there a place or experience you know about that brings you closer to God? Is there something you do or a place you go where you feel you can more clearly hear His voice? If so, where is that?

If not, you may want to experiment a little to see where it is that your heart begins to come alive. Write out a few thoughts of where it might be.

Links for the Week

www.surrenderedanduntamed.com/promise

Below you will find a list of links that exist purely for your pleasure. If you enjoyed the first chapter of the DVD and want to see more, learn more, and maybe even laugh a little, type in the links you see below. Just to give you an idea of what you will see, we have written out a few notes here.

When Alex was in Antarctica, he had a small camera with him that he used for his daily journal/diary. The only way to begin to understand what he went through while in Antarctica is to watch his daily journals. They are fun, miserable, random, and just a little insane. The first ten such diary entries are at the link below:

www.surrenderedanduntamed.com/alexdiary1

Antarctica is known for its fierce and sudden storms. Four hours after Alex and Sibu's landing on a natural ice runway, a massive storm descended with lightning speed. Check it out at the link below:

www.surrenderedanduntamed.com/firststorm

Alex and his cameraman took hundreds of stunning pictures while in Antarctica. Check out a few of them at the link below:

www.surrenderedanduntamed.com/pictures

In case you have forgotten about the link we already mentioned in the introduction—if you want to see what it takes to land a massive Russian Ilyushin (airplane) on a natural ice runway in Antarctica in high winds . . . check it out here!

www.surrenderedanduntamed.com/landing

Experiences

S&U Experience 1—The Book

Enjoy the excerpt below, taken from Jason's book, *Surrendered and Untamed: A Field Guide for the Vagabond Believer*.

The Polar Express

I was sitting in the theatre beside a three-year-old boy named Ethan Wilde. Ethan is my son. We were about to watch *The Polar Express*. I was a little distracted because we had just moved to North Carolina. We were pretty sure God had asked us to. Pretty sure. We had spent our savings and were now digging into our "good credit." We were beyond strapped, and spending eight bucks for the afternoon matinee caused that voice in my head to say, *Are you crazy?*

A thirty-year-old man with a wife and two kids isn't usually 100 percent certain of much, but I was about 97 percent sure I was to spend all my time and resources birthing a ministry. I would later find out that this was a lifestyle and that my true ministry was simply believing God. He had told me to believe, to stay the course. But as the money flew out of our bank account, I was more than worried. I was scared.

Dave Ramsey's evaluation would have been . . . uh, financial suicide. Now, I know Dave Ramsey has saved many people from financial ruin. But this was between me and another Savior; it had nothing to do with financial responsibility. This was about irresponsible, unsound, downright foolish obedience. I'll return to this a little later. . . .

20

Back to *The Polar Express*. If you haven't seen it, try to; it's wonderful. It's about a young boy who, while growing up, loses his ability to believe in God—I mean Santa Claus. Fortunately, Jesus, the Holy Spirit, and God—I mean three variations of Tom Hanks—band together to guide the boy back into believing. I realize that sounds confusing, but stick with me.

It's Christmas Eve and instead of dreaming of the best day of the year, the boy is in his bedroom agonizing over the universal question: Does God . . . sorry, I mean Santa Claus . . . really exist? He used to believe, but now in the mind of this blossoming adult, a fat, bearded, jolly man delivering presents to the entire world's population in one night seems impossible. Add in flying reindeer, elves, a North Pole toy factory—it all seems completely foolish. The boy is in danger of becoming a realist.

And then a deep rumbling. It grows louder until it fills his room and even jumps out into our theatre seats. Like an earthquake, it shakes and rattles his shelf of sports trophies. The boy crawls over to his window, peers out and what to his wondering eyes should appear? An enormous train decked in his front yard.

Dressed in his pajamas and rubber rain boots, he cautiously walks out to the train and meets Jesus . . . I'm sorry, I mean a train conductor played by Tom Hanks. The conductor says, "Well . . . are you coming?"

That's a question worth remembering.

This amazes the boy. He really wants to get on the train, but at the same time, the idea terrifies him. Finally, as the train begins to inch forward, his heart wins out and he takes the outstretched hand of the conductor.

And so the journey begins, a grand adventure filled with mountaintops and frozen lakes and howling wolves and dancing waiters balancing hot chocolate. It's exciting and dangerous all at the same time. Along the way the boy meets the Holy Spirit . . . I'm sorry, I mean a ghost who oddly resembles Tom Hanks.

21

After several breathtaking moments, the train reaches its destination—the North Pole. There are elves everywhere, and music, dancing, and singing. It is truly a magical place. I'd like to go there someday.

Everyone is awaiting Santa's arrival, which signals the official start of Christmas. The elves are singing Christmas songs. Some are whispering, "Is he here?" and some are yelling, "Do you see him?" The anticipation is almost unbearable.

The reindeer harnessed to Santa's sleigh are going wild! Their master is coming! They can sense it! The sleigh bells are ringing and all who believe in Santa can hear them, their pristine crystal tones adding to the beautiful, chaotic anticipation. The children that made the journey are there too. The air is electric.

And then there is the boy. He had all but decided that Santa is not real and yet wants—with his whole heart—to be wrong. Surrounded by a sea of believers, the boy dares to hope; in fact, hope is everywhere, and it's contagious.

A slow hush falls on the crowd, and all eyes become focused on a building at the end of the square. The doors burst open. There is a bright light and within the doorframe a silhouette. Suddenly the whole square erupts. "There he is!" shouts an elf. "I see him!" says one of the girls, but the boy, pressed by the crowd, can't see and still can't hear the sleigh bells. Why can't he hear? Desperate, he jumps and presses his way through the sea of elves to the front. And then, there He is, God . . . I'm sorry, I mean Santa Claus, who is also played by Tom Hanks. . . .

Suddenly the boy hears everything: the bells, the worshiping elves, the celebrating kids, the dancing reindeer. And I'm sitting beside my son, and I'm desperately trying to hide my face from the little girl next to me. Why? 'Cause I'm bawling my eyes out and whispering, "I believe, I believe, I believe . . . I love You, Lord, and I believe . . ."

I've been given a promise from God. But sometimes holding on to it can be rather difficult. Life moves along, things happen; the world is a very busy and noisy place. It's easy to wake up one day and find you're just not sure anymore. Believing has become a lost art and the promise has become a mountain that seems unscalable. In fact, it has often seemed, the harder I try to summit, the farther the peak is from me. But I'm convinced that the "God-lived life" is one of learning *how* to believe. It's learning how to cling to God and keep His promises alive in your heart.

In the movie it took the conductor, the ghost, and Santa working together to woo the child. One man played all three characters, a trinity working in unison, until ultimately the boy made the decision to believe. The boy's heart had wanted to believe from the very start. And that desire was enough to push him into the perilous journey.

Consider the possibility that God is asking you the very same question: *Well . . . are you coming?*

Excerpt taken from *Surrendered and Untamed:
A Field Guide for the Vagabond Believer*,
Chapter 1—The Promise

S&U Experience 2—The Album

"My Beautiful Song" is track number 1 on the *Surrendered & Untamed* album and really captures the message of this chapter best. It's about awakening to the revolutionary love of God—learning to live fully alive, always moving forward, always believing God's promises and engaging them. It's about releasing our lives into His beautiful song. Check it out here:

www.surrenderedanduntamed.com/beautifulsong

My Beautiful Song

I felt a sense of urgency, a lion come alive in me in revelation
  of Your love
It's time to claim the world, to live life true and wild, a revolution of my heart
Please be all I need, please, my heart begs, please be all I need
If life were a song, come, Savior, come, sing in me . . . a beautiful song

My beautiful song, my life fully sung, Your beautiful song

There's a cry in my spirit so loud you can hear it, my soul's
  awakening
I want to see as You see, I want to dream what You dream, to
  be what You made me
So let my joy or tears be worship to Your ears, as a sweet
  melody
To join the everlasting song, come, Savior, come, sing in me

I want to live this life in the brilliance of Your song
I want to worship You with a life fully sung . . . a beautiful
  song
My beautiful song, my life fully sung, Your beautiful song
Sing, Jesus, sing in me . . .

S&U Experience 3—The Film

As my mom always says, "All work, introspection, deep thinking,
and no play leads to a month of less fun and possible headaches."
I guess she doesn't say that, but it could be true. For those of you
who have access to the internet and want to meet Alex's expedition
partner, you will want to continue reading. If you don't have internet
access, no worries, you can still contemplate the question and then go
grab an ice cream or something—this is supposed to be fun, after all!

Before Alex Harris took his first step onto the Antarctic continent,
he spent an entire year training at his home in South Africa. It didn't

matter that he had already climbed the seven summits (the highest mountains on every continent), as well as accomplished countless other physical feats; he never took those things for granted. He never rested on past victories.

He spent countless hours training with his expedition partner, Sibusiso Vilane. Alex knew that if he didn't fully prepare for the expedition, he probably would not make it back alive.

Watch the clip below and spend a few moments contemplating the fact that it is nearly impossible for Alex to engage his promise on his own. Do you have someone in your life who can encourage the promises of God in you?

www.surrenderedanduntamed.com/meetsibu

2

Risk

Live in such a way that unless God shows up, what you're attempting to do is bound to fail. This is the nature of the Gospel.

—Bill Johnson, author and pastor

Introduction

Last week you watched as Alex Harris took his first steps on his journey across Antarctica. His eyes lit up with an excitement and passion that was palpable. Alex had spent years dreaming about and working toward this expedition, and finally he was able to begin. However, like all journeys that are worth taking, Alex soon learned that his dreams didn't even come close to the reality of what was required to accomplish this trek. Though he had trained and prepared in every way he knew how, there was nothing he could have done to fully prepare him for what was to come.

This is the nature of every great story; it's the nature of every journey worth taking. It all starts with a dream, with a promise, but a promise without action is like a seed that never gets planted. A dream is wonderful—it's what gets us off the couch—and it's in the middle of those all-important first steps that we begin to engage our promise. It's also in the middle of those first steps that the reality of the dream begins to sink in. Is it scary? Yes. But to attempt a journey that doesn't at least scare us a little isn't a journey worth taking. Besides, sometimes what scares us can also be the thing that most excites us. Sometimes, scary can be fun.

Icebreaker

Before you watch the video for today, take a moment to get to know everyone in the group a little more. We don't want you to share your dreams or your most embarrassing moments and we don't want you to talk about what you did this week or what you hope to do next week—we'll get to that later. Right now we want you to do something . . . shallower.

Everyone has a hidden talent—yes, everyone. It may be that you know how to juggle or maybe you can touch your nose with your tongue. We are pretty sure that you can do something that is either interesting or just plain silly. Take a few minutes to go around the room and share your talents.

Ponderings

Take a moment to read through the section below. Write your answer to the question in the space provided.

Risk can look like many different things. The word *risk* can apply to something that is physical, such as embarking on a trek to the South Pole. There are emotional or relational risks, such as telling

28

someone you love them when you have no idea how they feel about you. Risk can also be applied to your spiritual life. For some, risk simply looks like sharing your testimony; for others, it's giving in a way you have never given before. This kind of risk is called faith. It's about believing in ways you never have before. It's about stepping out and trusting God will restore, or provide, or heal, and so on.

The fact is, if you have asked Jesus into your heart, you have already risked, you have already trusted. But the question is, have you continued to risk? Do you continue to step out?

Do you think of yourself as a risk taker? If so, in what area of life are you risking and trusting? And what areas of life do you tend to shy away from when it comes to risking and trusting?

 ## DVD

Now, it's time for the big moment: what happens to Alex next? Will he keep believing while in Antarctica? Will he get frostbite, see penguins, and finally . . . change his underwear? Put in the DVD, find the chapter titled "Risk," press Play, and find out!

In an instant, my mind internalized what this meant. It was the 5-kilometer-long crevasse and I was standing on the middle of it on a snow bridge—and it had held.

–Alex

Jesus did not die on the cross just to keep us safe; He died to make us dangerous. Don't let fear dictate your decisions. Live courageously for the cause of Christ.

—Mark

29

Live in such a way that unless God shows up,
what you're attempting to do is bound to fail.
This is the nature of the Gospel.

—Bill Johnson

Group Discussion

Take some time to discuss the video with the group.

1. Was there a moment, a scene, or something Alex or Mark said that stood out to you regarding your own journey?

2. Read the section below and then discuss the final group question:

   One of the more memorable moments in the DVD is when Alex Harris takes the cup of boiling water and throws it into the air. The water immediately turns to vapor because the air is so desperately cold. When he throws the water, Alex says,

   > The Bible speaks about our lives being nothing more than vapor. That glass of boiling water, that's what our lives are like. Vapor. Potential. And only when we cast it to God and His plans can we actually change this world and bring about the kind of place that God wants for us.

   Alex was talking about James 4:14, which says

   > You don't know the first thing about tomorrow. You're nothing but a wisp of fog, catching a brief bit of sun before disappearing. (Message)

30

Every person is filled with infinite potential. That's because God is living within us. But how do we practically "cast our lives to God"? How do we trust on a daily basis?

3. Also, Alex's statement above says that we can change this world and bring about the kind of place God wants for us. What would that look like in your life?

Meditation

Take 5–10 minutes to write your thoughts in response to the questions below. When everyone is done, if you still have time, go around the group one last time and be ready to share just one of your answers.

1. Being close to God is the safest place anyone could ever be. Yet the way God defines the word *safe* may not be the way we understand it. We tend to see *safe* as interchangeable with *comfortable*. However, God defines it in a very different way.

> Fear not, for I am with you.
>
> —God
> Isaiah 43:5 ESV

"God with us" means we can live a life without fear, but this verse in Isaiah implies that we will be in uncomfortable situations where there is cause for fear. This verse implies that a life surrendered to God will lead us into "unsafe" places.

31

Our safety is found in obedience to the heart of God, and our comfort is found in His never-ending love. It's not a safety that guarantees long life and no hardships; it's a safety that establishes God's kingdom on earth through trusting believers.

Following God and engaging our promises is about radically surrendering all that we are and then stepping boldly into an untamed kind of believing. It takes a step of faith to engage our promise. It's a step that is often uncomfortable and even a little scary—it's called risk and it's the only way we begin to see our promise engaged.

So finally, we arrive at the question—

What are the areas in your life in which you fear? Write them below and take a moment to give them to God.

Now look at each one and ask Him how you can believe—how you can apply your faith through stepping out and risking. Write that down as well.

2. "Be strong and courageous" (Josh. 1:6).

When do I risk? How do I risk? Most of us do our best to avoid risk because, well, it's risky. Risk is what releases us into our promise. When we begin to define what it is God has for us, it's time to take the first step. That first step should be both scary and fun.

Embracing our promise means we are willing to step out into what at first may appear impossible. When we trust like this, when we surrender our lives, we put ourselves in a place where God can meet us and make the impossible possible.

Today, what does that first step look like?

 ## Links for the Week

www.surrenderedanduntamed.com/risk

Alex and his partner Sibu experienced miserable conditions throughout the journey. Some days the risk seemed almost too much. You can check out many entries of both of their video diaries via the link below.

www.surrenderedanduntamed.com/diary2

Antarctica is one of the more extreme places in the world. The temperatures can drop to −30° in the summer without the wind chill factor. In this week's video you watched as Alex threw a cup of boiling water high into the air. It immediately vaporized and dissipated. While on the frozen continent, Alex and his partner Sibu had a lot of fun with this and threw the boiling water into the air multiple times. Below is a link to a little montage that we like to call "rainmaker."

www.surrenderedanduntamed.com/rainmaker

Alex, Sibu, and their cameraman (me, Joel) took hundreds of stunning pictures while in Antarctica. Check out a few of them at the link below.

www.surrenderedanduntamed.com/pictures2

Because Alex had to carry all of his supplies with him on his expedition, he was very careful about how many extra supplies he brought with him. He made the choice to bring only one extra pair of underwear, which we all think is slightly disgusting. Check out the magical day when he was able to change them at the link below.

www.surrenderedanduntamed.com/underwear

Alex Harris is not some simple jock who just flexes muscles and feels no pain. I hate to say it, but Alex is also a poet and a published author. I hate to say it because it doesn't seem fair that Alex should have more than one great talent. Regardless, below is a link to a couple of his poems from a book of poetry that is as of yet untitled.

www.surrenderedanduntamed.com/poetry

 Experiences

S&U Experience 1—The Book

Enjoy the excerpt below, taken from Jason's book, *Surrendered and Untamed: A Field Guide for the Vagabond Believer.*

Scary Is Fun

We were on vacation in the wild Northwest. Vancouver Island, to be specific. My daughter Maddy was almost three years old. We were at the deep end of the local public indoor pool and she was on the diving board. It was at least as far away from the water as she was tall, and she was tall for her age. It had been her idea to jump and had seemed like a good idea from the shallow end. I waited in the water right below the diving board encouraging her, but to no avail. It was "too high" and "too scary."

Earlier in the week I had gone cliff jumping, a good seventy-five feet of it. I love rivers and have an unwavering opinion that they were created for my enjoyment. So when I see a river, I generally want to get in it. How I get in it is where the fun begins.

Pete, a good friend from the area, and I had hiked out to the river and spent about an hour swimming at the bottom of its beautiful 75-foot waterfall. After we finished swimming, we began the climb back up the trail. The trail sawbacked the side of the falls and we arrived at the top just in time to watch dumbfounded as a guy jumped into the water below.

Both Pete and I have done some cliff jumping in our day, but when we first saw the falls, we hadn't even considered it—it was really high. But once I saw the guy's head pop out of the water, I realized it could be done without dying. And so while Pete, with his back to me, talked to one of the jumper's friends at the cliff edge, I talked to myself.

"It's just two steps and you're over the edge." My eyes focused on the edge. "Just two steps." I took a deep breath. "Just two steps." I removed my shoes. "Just two steps." I took off my shirt. "Just two steps." I took another breath and then I took the two steps, and as I dropped, I sensed Pete turn and I heard him say, "Oh, Jason!"

It was an amazing experience and also a great story. One Pete and I have told and relived in the telling many times since. You see, Pete is not one to watch someone else get a good story without him. Within ten seconds, he had followed me over the edge. I still smile when picturing him eye rolling and muttering under his breath while quickly removing his shoes and shirt and then taking those two steps.

When we got back to the hotel, Maddy heard our stories. Now, it's hard to explain to a three-year-old why anyone would jump off a cliff. Three-year-olds don't have the capacity to understand this. The best I could do by way of explanation is "Sometimes, scary is fun."

So as I treaded water under the diving board, I reminded her again. "Honey, sometimes scary is fun!" She was a hard sell, but I persisted until we finally came to an agreement—I would jump with her. So I joined her on the diving board. "It's just two steps."

I would love to tell you that it wasn't too high, that her head didn't go under, and that there was nothing but joy in her eyes. But that would be a lie. The truth is, Maddy kept a death grip on me until we reached the side of the pool; she was convinced she had made a mistake. But once we got there, safe, she began to laugh with the wonder of the whole experience. I did too.

My little girl beat the diving board. Yes, it was too scary and too high, but she did it anyway. She jumped—for herself, for me, for the story. Years later, most of that vacation has faded from her memory, but the story of the diving board lives on. And "scary is fun" has become a household phrase.

Now let me give you a father's perspective. Before and after she jumped, I was enthusiastic in my encouragement. When we reached the side of the pool, I was immersed in her joy. For the rest of the week I was overwhelmed with pride. She had believed; she had lived fully and I got to be a part of it. I was her catalyst, her savior, and her friend. And together we beat the diving board. The wonder of my daughter's trust and then the opportunity to be faithful with it are a father's dream come true. If she had not jumped, we both would have missed out. But she did jump and now she owns that story. She owns that experience. And the diving board no longer controls her fear.

It's a great story.

Excerpt taken from *Surrendered and Untamed: A Field Guide for the Vagabond Believer*, Chapter 5—Do It for the Story

S&U Experience 2—The Album

"When the Stars Fall Like Rain" is a song about believing. There are moments where we must decide to believe, and that decision will define the rest of our lives. Even if we miss it, God invites us to step out and believe again. He has promises for us that can only be received through risking everything and taking the next step.

www.surrenderedanduntamed.com/starsfall

When the Stars Fall Like Rain

God was looking on me battered by the wind,
To see if I would stumble, to see if I would bend
I've said You're the son of God and I've forced water from a
    stone
And I've searched my heart's ruins till Your heart was found

And it's easy to seek passion and it's simple to give in
And it's in between these places that I'm tempted to live
I was born to bring You Glory and I was born to sing Your
    fame
From my hilltop to my valley I'm surrendered and untamed

Don't always know where we are going but it's just a matter
    of time
And I know with my next heartbeat it's this moment that
    decides
So give me the land of giants and give me the other side
For I am Your believer and we won't be denied

I saw the stars today, they rained down beautiful
Then Your glory came, revival for my soul
I saw the stars today and then Your glory came

I believe in revolution, love's not an institution
I believe in revelation, it's Your Spirit's inspiration
I believe the stars are falling, every one a seed of fire
And I believe a wave is coming to birth a holy pure desire

When the stars fall like rain
When the stars fall like rain . . .

S&U Experience 3—The Film

Alex Harris grew up a middle-class white African in Johannesburg, South Africa. He was too young to know what was happening with the apartheid government and was relatively sheltered in the then all-white city. His climbing and expedition partner Sibusiso Vilane grew up as an uneducated goat herder in South Africa's close neighbor, Swaziland. Through many years and multiple expeditions, Alex and Sibu have become close friends, though their cultures and backgrounds still played a larger role in their relationship than either of them initially realized. Check out some of the cultural issues that arose while they were on this insane journey across Antarctica at the link below.

www.surrenderedanduntamed.com/culture

3

The Wilderness

I think wilderness is different for everyone. Wilderness simply speaks of a season in our lives where things that hold meaning are distant from us.

—Alex

Introduction

You have already watched the previous two chapters of this four-part epic journey across Antarctica. Chapter 1 showed explorer Alex Harris take his first steps into the frozen wasteland and begin to lay hold of a promise God had given him when he was a child. The second chapter highlighted many of the problems that immediately surfaced as he boldly walked forward in faith.

In today's segment Alex continues his journey toward the South Pole. Will he make it before his supplies run out? Will the storms keep him from moving or cause his frostbite to worsen? Will Alex give up his dream and turn back toward base camp? Will Alex become angry with God or choose to believe no matter the circumstances?

Our prayer is that you will enjoy this session, laugh together, and experience God on a deeper and more intimate level.

Icebreaker

You will notice that the page next to this page is completely blank on both sides. That's not because we are just trying to make the guide look bigger—at least, not entirely. We actually have big plans for this page. Follow the three steps below!

1. If you fancy yourself an artist, or if you can draw a good stick-man . . . or if you breath oxygen, draw a picture. Your drawing should incorporate Alex Harris, a polar bear (no, polar bears don't live in Antarctica—yes, it's a better picture with one in it), a rookery of penguins (or just one or two), and the setting should be the plains of Antarctica. Go! Have fun.
2. Now, rip out your page and hand it into the group leader.

"WHAT!? RIP OUT A PAGE?!?"

Just imagine you are one of Robin Williams's students in *Dead Poets Society*. Go ahead and stand up on your chair, couch, desk, pew, coffee table, and rip away! (Don't get carried away, though; just rip the one page.) Now hand it to your group leader and he or she will mix them up so you can all vote on them, placing them into one of three categories:

- A. Brilliant! You are a da Vinci!
- B. Funny! You should do stand-up!
- C. Maybe you're a musician?

3. After you have voted, we would love it if your leader would scan the winning drawing for each category and send them to us. Also remind him or her to let us know from which part of the world you hail, and the name of your church.

We plan to post the best overall drawings on our website. We will also choose our favorite group drawings and announce a winner online. If your group drawings win, we will send your leader five free copies of the *Surrendered and Untamed* DVD, book, and CD. You also get one million dol—

Never mind. I just checked the budget. You just get the DVDs, books, and CDs.

Go to www.surrenderedanduntamed.com/drawing to see more details.

Ponderings

Take a moment to read through the section below before watching the film.

We have been invited to engage in the most amazing story ever told. It's dangerous and it's beautiful. It's rarely easy and sometimes scary, inspiring, and fulfilling. And all along the way, the question remains the same—will you believe?

It is a believing heart that will allow you to take one step, which turns into another, which turns into another, until at some point you find yourself in a place where there is no going back, and the only way to keep moving is to experience the miraculous intervention of God. Believing doesn't make for an easy life; it doesn't make difficulties go away. It simply changes your heart so that even in the midst of the wilderness seasons you see your situation through God's eyes.

Before pushing Play, write down what you are believing for today. Maybe you are in a wilderness season and need a miracle. Write it down. Maybe you are believing on someone else's behalf. Write that down.

DVD

Put in the DVD, find the chapter titled *The Wilderness*. Now go get your popcorn and soda, or your coffee and chocolate cake, or your edamame and spinach smoothie. Turn down the lights, get comfy, press Play, and enjoy!

━━━━━━

The wilderness is the place where we come to terms with who we are, and maybe more importantly, who we're not. It's the place where we truly surrender our lives to God.

—Mark

We want God to change our circumstances, but God wants to change our hearts.

—Mark

God whispers to us in our pleasures, speaks to us in our conscience, but shouts in our pains; it is His megaphone to rouse a deaf world.

—C. S. Lewis

 Group Discussion

Take some time to discuss the video with the group.

1. Was there a moment, a scene, or something Alex or Mark said that stood out to you regarding your own journey?

2. Was there anything that Alex or Mark said that you connected with? Why?

3. Have someone read the following quote and paragraph aloud. In the film Alex says, *"I think wilderness for everyone is different. . . . [Wilderness] simply speaks of a season in our lives where things that hold meaning are distant from us."*

   I (Mark) think Alex's definition of the wilderness is brilliant. In the DVD I talked about trying to start a church. I did all the work. I planned, I prepped, and I even opened a bank account. And then, in a relatively quick amount of time, all of my plans fell apart. We never even had our first meeting! I was heartbroken. Everything I believed I was supposed to do came crashing down. Have you experienced this? Are you experiencing this right now?

   Now take a moment to go around the group, giving everyone an opportunity to share a story about a season in which they

45

experienced the wilderness and how God came through. Focus on how God answered your prayers; on how he met you in the wilderness. Believing starts here, in remembering His goodness, His faithfulness.

After everyone has had a chance to share, take a moment to pray for each other, especially those who may be in a wilderness season right now. Start by thanking God for his never-ending love. Then ask Him for wisdom in how to pray. Ask God to reveal His presence—His heart—in your lives and for each situation. Ask for peace and strength.

Finally, ask God to begin to meet the seeming impossibilities. Believing can also be expressed in how we pray. We've already asked for wisdom; now we must begin to express what comes to mind about the situations we are praying for. Begin to believe in the God who works all things for good to those who love Him (Rom. 8:28). Feel free to wait on God, there is no rush. He may give you some further wisdom on how to pray.

If you spent a little extra time praying for each other, that's called church and it's nothing but good! If you still have time, take a moment to read through the meditation below. If you are out of time, try to find a moment this week to meditate on the thoughts below.

Meditation

Take 5–10 minutes to read through and meditate on the message below. When everyone is done, go around the group one last time and be ready to read/share your thoughts.

In the DVD, Alex compared a wilderness season to a physical wasteland. Here are some of his quotes.

My body was nothing, I could offer no resistance to this stupid sled.

It felt like the emptiness around us had robbed everything in my mind and my heart, that I was left now as empty as the land that we found ourselves in. And very quickly I sensed my head being assaulted by negative thoughts.

It made me mad. There were days when, I was like, "Lord, I understand that this is about suffering and in this I'm developing perseverance and my faith is being stretched, but how much must I suffer? Surely we've suffered enough!" And honestly, I shouted that out to the gloom sometimes: "Lord, how much more must I suffer?"

Have you ever felt this way?

In the midst of Alex's journey there is a pivotal moment where he has a revelation. He says, *"I thought, I'm going to pray enough that the Lord will change the weather,"* and Alex cried out with everything he had for God to change it. But he felt God say to him, *"You are praying about the wrong stuff . . . I brought you to this place because of this weather, but I can change your heart."*

At that moment Alex chose to begin to see his circumstance from heaven's perspective—God's point of view. Alex goes on to tell us, *"If my focus was on believing what God was saying, then I wouldn't be thinking so much of the problem, I would be thinking about my purpose."*

Alex chose to align his heart with God's, to see his circumstances from God's perspective. This led him to a faith that sustained him through the remainder of the journey.

47

To engage our promise we must see it through the eyes of God. We must step into a greater intimacy with Jesus. We must know Him— the sound of His voice, the works of His hand, and the beating of His heart. We must trust Him fully. And this is especially important when we are in the wilderness season.

I cannot afford to have a thought in my head about me that is not His.

—Bill Johnson, *When Heaven Invades Earth*

The truth found in this quote also applies to our wilderness season. Today, ask God to help you begin to see your wilderness, or the wilderness of your family or friends, from His perspective. Ask Him to reveal His heart to you.

 ## Links for the Week

www.surrenderedanduntamed.com/wilderness

We like to think many of the clips linked to below would make it onto a director's cut of the DVD. If you enjoyed this week's chapter in the DVD and want to dive further into Alex's insane journey, check out these links. If you didn't enjoy the film, well, why continue to torture yourself?

The DVD and guide have broken Alex and Sibu's journey down into four parts. We also have broken down their diaries into four parts. Check out part 3 of their on-camera diaries at the link below.

www.surrenderedanduntamed.com/diary3

Alex and Sibu were in Antarctica through the month of December, so they ended up having quite a lonely Christmas together. One of the most sincere diary cam moments, and in our minds one of the funniest moments as well, is when Alex decides to sing to his wife.

Below you will find a link to the unedited version of his song. Touching and hilarious all at the same time!

www.surrenderedanduntamed.com/christmas

I (Joel) was in Antarctica filming this S&U series and I was only supposed to be there for a couple weeks. The plan was to get all of the long-distance shots of Alex and Sibu trekking across the frozen plains in the first two weeks. We would then use those shots for the entire series. Because Antarctica generally looks the same no matter when you go, this seemed like the best idea. The problem was, the day I planned to fly out, a massive storm descended—it lasted eleven days. This made air travel in and out impossible. The downside—I spent eleven extra days living in a tent in Antarctica. The upside—I was able to get a ton of extra amazing footage.

www.surrenderedanduntamed.com/thestorm

Initially, for this series, we planned on having Alex do a little more teaching—we thought it would be great if he shared some of the truths right there in Antarctica. However, no matter how we edited it, we were unable to make Alex the explorer and Alex the teacher flow together seamlessly. In the end we took out almost all of the actual teaching sections and ended with what we have now. That being said, there were a few great moments that were tough for me to take out of the final edit. Below is one such clip.

www.surrenderedanduntamed.com/beach

We had a great time filming with Mark in Death Valley, Nevada. We spent two long days in the insanely hot desert, burning our feet and laughing a lot. Below is a look at some of the more fun moments of the shoot.

www.surrenderedanduntamed.com/batterson

Alex attempted to summit Mount Everest on three separate occasions. On the first two attempts, he came close to the summit but was turned back before his dream could become a reality. On both attempts he nearly died. At the link below, Alex tells one of his stories of being inside his tent on the side of the mountain when a massive storm descended. This story will give you shivers—when you are ready to watch this video, take a deep breath, sit back, and hold on!

www.surrenderedanduntamed.com/zipper

 Experiences

S&U Experience 1—The Book

Enjoy the excerpt below taken from Jason's book, *Surrendered and Untamed: A Field Guide for the Vagabond Believer.*

Wilderness

We were "shelved"—it was over and I couldn't believe it. My whole adult life had been given to the band. All those hockey dreams of me never getting to play came crashing home. I was miserable. It felt like I had been dragged into the wilderness, that place of disappointment, sorrow, and pain, where time itself seems to have forgotten you.

The next several years I lived in a spiritual wasteland much like the famed wilderness in the Bible where the Israelites spent forty years just hanging out. God was there with manna and water but not much else.

50

Before this season, I used to dread the idea of the wilderness; it was something to be avoided at all costs. But over the course of several years, I came to understand that if we breathe, we will experience wilderness seasons in life. Whether it's the loss of a loved one, a career derailed, or just a season of waiting, it's usually something we have little to no control over. What's crazy is that the wilderness season often comes right on the heels of receiving the promise.

I think many of us have experienced this phenomenon. We receive God's promise and then get "shelved." It's nothing new. If you look at the heroes in the Bible, most of them spent years on the shelf. Joseph, Moses, David— they all spent time "herding sheep" after the promise of God had been established in their hearts. They all did time in the wilderness.

In fact, Jesus Himself modeled this for us. After His baptism, He comes out of the water to a voice that shakes the heavens: "This is my beloved Son, with whom I am well pleased." A dove descends and the Spirit of God rests on Him. Jesus' promise is made public.

At this point I would have expected Him to step out of the water and begin His signs and wonders, find men to disciple and miracles to do. Instead, Jesus steps out of the water, follows the Holy Spirit into the wilderness, and models for us what it's like to embrace your promise.

What is most amazing about this story is that it was God who led Jesus into the wilderness. The Bible tells us Jesus did nothing apart from His heavenly Father. He lived out the perfect will of God; Jesus willingly went into the wilderness.

I spent the first part of my life learning about my unique promise and the most recent part learning how to surrender it. I'm learning that the extent to which I possess my promise is directly linked to the measure

51

of my surrender. Strangely, to truly participate in my promise now, I need to surrender it, and that's where the wilderness comes into play.

It's the wilderness that prepares our hearts. In the wilderness we learn to surrender our understanding of the promise. And in this surrender, we begin to see our promise through God's eyes. This is absolutely essential if we want to fully embrace our promise.

I now believe that the wilderness is the place where our relationship with God can be developed. This is a place where He can daily meet with us and provide for our needs. Where He can stretch and increase our capacity to believe with Him. Even in the midst of disappointment, sorrow, or pain, the wilderness can become a place of trust, beauty, and surrender. A place where we can meet God face-to-face and know His love, His grace, His kindness, and His goodness. It's one of the places where God can deepen our reve-lation of who He is in connection to where He wants to take us.

I wonder: if we were to go straight to the promise without the wilderness, would we believe enough to embrace the promise?

That being said, we must remember the wilderness is not our home. It is not our promise. It is not the end of the story. I know from experience that if believing wanes in the wilderness, you begin to settle there, thinking, *This must be as good as it gets.*

I'm afraid many Christians in wilderness seasons have stopped believing and taken up permanent resi-dence, mistaking the wilderness for the Promised Land. There is nothing wrong with wilderness living as long as we understand it is not our home. There is so much more; we cannot settle there.

Excerpt taken from *Surrendered and Untamed: A Field Guide for the Vagabond Believer,* Chapter 3—Monday Morning

S&U Experience 2—The Album

There is available to us, through believing while in the wilderness, a profound intimacy with God. A sweet trust, a beautiful strength, a lovely surrender where God meets with us and begins to merge our heart with His until we begin to dream His dreams and see as He sees. This season of absolute surrender releases us into the untamed believing. This song, "Only Dead Men Can Go," is the journey from surrender to untamed.

www.surrenderedanduntamed.com/deadmen

Only Dead Men Can Go

So sweet to trust in Jesus
And take Him at His word
And rest upon His promise
Oh for grace to trust Him more

I came believing with righteous intent
To lay hold of innocence
I climbed the mountain, got on my knees
Until revival made a home inside of me
A perfect fear claimed my soul, said
This is a place only dead men can go

No risk without danger, No faith if I'm sure
I'm not but I'm absolutely positive in the way I'll live
Surrendered and untamed, whole and insane
For Your glory, it's Your story working in me
The sweet mystery of Your love—hallelujah, I believe

It's begun and is finished, a revolution of the cross
I've awakened to a movement, love my burden, the birthplace
    of holiness
So rise up, oh bride of God, be faithful with your trust
It's heart and soul and mind and strength
In one song, worship the King—hallelujah, I believe . . .

I found my way up by the wonders of Your love
I found my way out in surrender to Your cross

Come, oh Glory, fill my heart, Come, oh Brilliance, fill my
sight
Every particle of me till I'm a portrait of Your grace
Love my burden, love rescue me

S&U Experience 3—The Film

If you have checked out any of the previous film experiences from the earlier chapters, you will have already met Sibusiso Vilane. Sibu was Alex's expedition partner on his trek to the South Pole as well as his climbing partner three years earlier when they climbed Mount Everest together. Sibu was born in Swaziland and is the first black man in the world to have climbed Mount Everest. While on the Antarctic expedition, Sibu's wife called him via his satellite phone and told him that his son was desperately sick. Sibu was stuck. There was no way to get home. He was only halfway through his expedition, and even if he called an emergency rescue plane, there was still no way to get off the continent. The winds were howling and no plane would be able to take them home for at least a couple more weeks.

Unable to go home and be with his son, Sibu did something truly amazing. He fasted all food for a full twenty-four hours. He pulled his sled across the frozen wasteland without any form of human fuel. During this truly miserable day, Sibu prayed for his son to get well. Go to the link below to see the whole story, meet Sibu's wife, and find out what happened to his son.

www.surrenderedanduntamed.com/fasting

4

Destiny

God said, "Don't come any closer. Remove your sandals from your feet. You're standing on holy ground."

Exodus 3:5 Message

Introduction

You have watched the previous three chapters of this four-part epic adventure series. Alex started this journey with a passion that was fueled by the promises of God. From the moment he took his first step, the reality of the journey began to set in. But believing God was with him, he remained determined even while experiencing the harsh and untamed wilderness. Alex continued to put one foot in front of the other—literally.

We have arrived at the final chapter. Will Alex make it to the South Pole or will he be attacked by rogue penguins? Will he accomplish his dream of standing on the southernmost tip of the world, or will he fall into a crevasse and never be heard from again? Will the cast of *Seinfeld* get together for a tenth season? Find the answers to these and many more burning questions in the dramatic conclusion to this first volume of *Surrendered and Untamed*.

Icebreaker

Take a moment to go around the group and talk about one of your "great moments" in life. Don't simply state the facts of what happened; relive the story so that the group can experience it with you. Getting married to the love of your life and bringing a child into the world are certainly highlight moments, but for today let's focus elsewhere. Think of something that you worked toward and then accomplished. It doesn't have to be something that happened recently; it could be something that happened when you were a child (e.g., scoring the winning goal in whatever sport you played). Remember, try to paint the picture, take a few minutes per person, and allow the group to feel, smell, and experience the moment with you. This is a great time to practice your storytelling skills!

Ponderings

Take a moment to read through the section below before watching the film.

When David stepped out on the battlefield to face Goliath, two vast armies were watching him. To the spectators, it appeared that David was just a boy, small and weak in comparison to Goliath. But David was living in faith and perceived a greater reality—God's reality. It's an unseen reality that has to be lived by faith. And in God's story, we are the giants.

It's time we came to an understanding of a higher reality, a greater truth. "Greater is He that is in me than he that is in the world" (see 1 John 4:4). We have barely scratched the surface of our glorious promise.

Before pushing Play, determine in your heart to believe His good love. He is for us, and our promise is true even if we can't see the fullness of it today.

It is time to step out on our battlefield—and claim our promise. It's time to live surrendered and untamed. It's time to wake the sleeping giant within. It's time to believe the unique promise He's given each and every one of us.

 DVD

Time for the big moment! We can imagine how you are feeling right now; this is like when *Return of the Jedi* opened. It's bigger than DiCaprio and Winslet's *Titanic*. It's probably been hard to concentrate or interact with your small group. We imagine the week has been agonizing, waiting for this final film. You have probably been dreaming about snow and ice and Alex . . . Well, the wait is over. Put in the DVD, find the chapter titled "Destiny," press Play, and enjoy!

It was that one step done over and over and over again that enabled us to get to the South Pole. That one step was probably the most important single part of the whole journey.

—Alex

*Claim the promise,
take the risk,
endure the wilderness, and
pursue the destiny.*
—Mark

57

As we let our own light shine, we unconsciously give other people permission to do the same.

—Marianne Williamson

 ## Group Discussion

Take some time to discuss the video with the group.

1. What are your first impressions?

2. Was there a moment, a scene, or something Alex or Mark said that stood out to you regarding your own journey?

3. Alex says,

> Success is not just about persevering every day . . . It's about managing all the little problems that threaten to escalate out of control and bring about certain failure. While there are little things, like a bit of frostbite, a broken ski, a hole in the tent . . . these things on their own aren't expedition destroyers, but if they are left unchecked, they can quickly run out of control.

How does this quote apply to your daily life?

4. In today's film, Mark makes the statement,

> Sometimes we fall into the when/then syndrome. When I get married, when I get my degree, my promotion, my raise . . . then I'll be happy. But if we wait to worship God until we get to the Promised Land, we're going to waste our life. We've got to worship Him right here, right now.

Do you feel like you've ever approached life with this mentality? If so, how do you think you can change this? What can you practically do that will allow you to see the hand of God in your life even in the midst of chaos?

When everyone has shared, feel free to worship together. You don't need to sing to worship. Just pray with thankfulness.

 ## Meditation

If you still have time, take a moment to read through the meditation below. When everyone is done, go around the group one last time

59

and share your heart. If you are out of time, try to find a moment this week to meditate on the thoughts below.

Alex says,

> People focus too much on the end goal in life more than they do on the steps that are required to achieve that end goal. . . . The temptation to look at [all the steps] is great, but in there is the very quick key to failure. . . . I think of it as the meaningful paradox. Most people in life tend to think of these little things as meaningless—one step. It was that one step done over and over and over again that enabled us to get to the South Pole.

In the first week of this guide we encouraged you to dream big. We encouraged you to remember how you used to dream when you were a child. Somewhere, whether hidden deep in your heart or bubbling along the surface of your soul, your promise is inside of you. We believe many people already have a pretty good idea of what their promise is. They already know a part of that thing that will bring them fully alive.

Yet, as Alex said in the quote above, they have focused on the end goal, they have looked at the insane amount of work and sacrifice that it would take to lay hold of their promise, and in so doing, the goal soon felt daunting and insurmountable—and this is a sure key to failure. Victory is found in knowing your promise and then taking one step at a time. God is not, nor has He ever been, a realist. God is the eternal optimist.

So finally . . . a question.

Make two lists below. The left side should be what the realist inside of you says; it would include some of the lies you have fallen for regarding your life. The right side should be what the believing heart, what faith, says. It's the "How does God think about me and my promise?" list. Spend some time on this. Maybe even come back to it when you are alone.

Here is an example to help you get started. The point is to see the lie and then embrace the truth.

The Realist	The Believing Heart
I can never travel or do missions, I simply don't have the money.	God has placed it in my heart to bring His love to the world. He will provide when I step out.

Today, confess to God areas where you may have been a realist. Begin to ask God for a faith that will grab hold of these promises. You serve a good God who wants to release His power in your life in greater ways than you can ask or imagine. The Bible tells us that the truth sets us free, and that's where we can begin to fully embrace our promise.

Links for the Week

www.surrenderedanduntamed.com/destiny

Below you will find a number of links that will take you to the *Surrendered and Untamed* website. These links will take you deeper into the world of S&U. Because of the constraints of time and format, we were unable to show the whole story of Alex and Sibusiso's trek to the South Pole. Many directors would be frustrated by this and sit around complaining to their friends that they had to cut some of the best scenes in the story. Once we finished doing that, we decided to give the publisher exactly what they want AND give you, the viewer, links to the best of what was cut—it's a win/win!

Now, the choice is yours. If you would like, check out the links below to extra footage from *Surrendered and Untamed*.

Alex and his partner Sibu were expected to perform on-camera diaries once a day, every day during their insane trek. When Alex returned home, he told me (Joel) that though they both promised to do so, in the end there were a few days where they were either too tired, angry, or uncaring to film yet another diary. I have been nice up till now because Alex and Sibu are close friends of mine. But now the gloves come off. Shame on you, both. Shame, shame, shame. The nerve of extreme explorers in subzero, life-threatening conditions!

Enjoy some of their video diaries at the link below.

www.surrenderedanduntamed.com/diary4

The beginning of this week's DVD chapter started with Alex telling a story about when he was in his early twenties and he was caught on the top of a Russian mountain in a lightning storm. While he was climbing, lightning struck, and literally forked above his head, killing the man directly in front of him as well as the man directly behind him. This is a horrible story that drastically changed the direction of Alex's life. We have placed the full, unedited story at the link below.

www.surrenderedanduntamed.com/electricstorm

Alex, Sibu, and I (Joel) took an amazing amount of still pictures on this expedition. Some of the pics made it into the final chapter on the DVD. Yet due to time constraints, many did not make the cut, but they're too amazing not to post somewhere. Take a look at some of the best pics across the frozen wonderland at the link below.

www.surrenderedanduntamed.com/pics3

You watched as Alex drank 100 ml (~ ½ cup) of olive oil and almost gagged while doing it. Both Alex and Sibu each drank 100 ml a day for 65 days because it was the only way they could consume a full 800 calories in such a small container. In order to trek unsupported to the South Pole, this means that they had to carry absolutely everything with them. Though they definitely would have preferred steak, they had to pick something light and compact. Some other teams who have trekked to the pole in the past have chosen to chew through a stick of butter every day. Both the olive oil and the butter are pretty disgusting, if you ask me. Check out Alex and Sibu's thoughts and reactions to the olive oil at the link below.

www.surrenderedanduntamed.com/oliveoil

Earlier in this guide we told you that Alex Harris is a published author as well as a poet. He has written most of his poetry while sitting in the shadow of some of the world's highest mountains and in the midst of some of his more dangerous experiences. He also wrote a few while on his trek across Antarctica. Check out some of his Antarctica-inspired poems at the link below.

www.surrenderedanduntamed.com/poetry2

At the link below, Alex recounts the first time he saw Everest with his own eyes. It was a powerful moment for a young man who had studied and dreamed and worked for years to get himself there. What amazes me is that from the ground, Alex looked up and immediately realized that, if he continued to gaze at the mountain, it would mean sure failure. He needed to climb the mountain one step at time and not dwell on the journey. Check out this powerful moment at the link below.

www.surrenderedanduntamed.com/eyesoff.com

Experiences

S&U Experience 1—The Book

Enjoy the excerpt below taken from Jason's book, *Surrendered and Untamed: A Field Guide for the Vagabond Believer*.

The Jump

I have a friend named Joel Carver. I just call him Carver. I think Carver is a pretty cool name, but that's beside the point. Carver is the kind of guy who just knows how to have fun, and he's not scared. I know this because every time we talk about doing something fun, he always says, "I'm not scared."

I had gone to Seattle to surprise my friend Carver for his birthday. His wife Tennille, Karen, and I had been planning the surprise for months. So when I showed up out of the blue, it didn't take long for both of us to decide we needed to do something amazing to mark this special occasion. Well, after a brief discussion, that "something" was obvious—tandem skydiving.

The day before we jumped, I was a nervous wreck. Any time I thought about it, I got queasy. Carver and I began to relate stories we had heard of other jumpers, and of course, eventually the talk turned to the horror stories until one of us would laugh nervously. Then Carver would give his famous phrase, "I'm not scared." Then we'd change the subject.

But once we arrived at the little shack out in the beautiful Northwest countryside, my feelings turned from nervous to excited.

So, as I signed the forms that essentially said, "If you die, or are terribly injured, we are sorry but you can't blame us because you're the idiot that wanted to jump out of an airplane in the first place," I wasn't nervous. As I put on the orange prisonlike jumpsuit, and my instructor strapped on my harness, I wasn't scared. In fact, I was giddy, joking and tee-hee-ing with Carver like an adolescent schoolgirl.

On the van ride over to the plane, I was practically humming with anticipation. And as I stood on the tarmac, I listened with a sense of exhilaration as my instructor ran through the last-minute details. When he mentioned the importance of keeping our arms and legs close to our body so that they wouldn't act as a windmill causing us to spin out of control, I fearlessly joked that we had nicknamed that phenomenon "the death spin."

For those who do not know, there have been times when a jumper begins to spin so violently that they lose control of their senses. They can begin to experience euphoria to such an extent that they actually lose track of time—when jumping out of an airplane, losing track of time is always a bad idea. They have actually found jumpers (landers?) with un-pulled parachutes, which is probably where that joke came from—"Parachute for sale, never been opened, small bloodstain."

When the eight of us climbed into the Volkswagen bug with wings, I was grinning from ear to ear. As we neared the end of the runway, I thought, "Here we go!"

The second we left earth, however, I experienced a terror beyond words. Honestly, if there had not been a girl on the plane, I would have peed myself. I'm not saying I did pee myself, I'm saying I would have if not for that girl . . .

It was a windy day and the takeoff was turbulent, to say the least. The earth disappeared beneath us at an alarming rate. I remember being consumed with two thoughts—first, "Is there any way I can get out of this?" and then, "Oh crap, the death spin." Still, I'm proud to say that I manned up and you couldn't see the terror on my face or hear it in my voice.

If the takeoff was traumatic, when the instructor told Carver and me to roll up the flimsy canvas flap that separated us from 11,000 feet of sky, I nearly had a seizure. At this point I vaguely remember my instructor pointing out the beautiful landscape below us.

"Look at the mountains! Aren't they beautiful?"

To which I responded, "Yeah, they are gorgeous!" But I couldn't see a thing.

My instructor kept yapping. "Look at the Seattle skyline, and the ocean, isn't it all amazing?"

"Shut up, just shut your stupid mouth!" I wanted to scream. But instead I graciously said, "Yeah, it's all amazing!" Still, I couldn't see squat.

Then the plane slowed down and my instructor told me to swing my feet out over the nothingness. *That's the stupidest idea I've ever heard! You are an idiot!* I thought to myself. But I robotically obeyed and whiteknuckled a bar on the inside of the plane. I remember hysterically grasping the irony of holding this bar to keep me from falling out when at any moment we were going to jump. Irony is always so ironic.

At this point my mind had exhausted every scenario in which I could get out of jumping and still retain my dignity. *What if the plane were to run out of gas?* I thought. *No, wait, that's not a good idea. What if I began to have a fake seizure . . . that's it! Great idea, Jason . . . no, wait . . . the fastest way to a hospital is what I'm trying to avoid. What if . . .* But no matter how hard I tried, I couldn't find a plausible way out of jumping. It was gonna happen!

Then the pilot shouted, "We missed the drop. I'm gonna take us around again!" The plane tilted, and for about five minutes I had to sit at the edge looking down at my toes, which at this point hung 11,000 feet over earth.

For the first minute I was in full panic. I started to wonder about my tandem instructor. I realized that I didn't know anything about him. I should have asked him some personal questions, like "How is your home life?" or "Have you been feeling depressed lately?" I was pretty sure it wasn't my time to check out, but I had no idea about my tandem instructor. I pictured myself in heaven, and Jesus asking, "What are you doing here?" "I'm with him," I would say, as I pointed at my instructor.

Plus, were we really strapped together? I mean, I think I felt it. I was 99 percent sure. No wait, 97 percent sure . . . 92 percent sure? . . . Well, you get the picture. I kept looking inside the plane at Carver and subtly pointing to my straps. But he didn't understand and I didn't want to yell, as I thought now was not the best time to upset my tandem instructor by questioning his competence.

Clearly I was about to lose it. Then Carver yelled, "Surrendered and untamed, baby!" And something happened—sorta like scales fell from my eyes. I took a deep breath and began to praise God. At that moment I experienced a peace that was absolutely at odds with my circumstance. Maybe even a peace that surpasses understanding. There on the edge of my demise, I worshiped. I realized this was something I had dreamed of doing my entire life. Here I was, 11,000 feet above earth, and even though I was terrified, there was peace. And it was then I saw the beautiful mountains, the ocean, the skyline.

My tandem instructor tapped my shoulder and we rocked back and forth once, twice—and suddenly I was skydiving.

Surrendered and untamed, baby!

Excerpt taken from *Surrendered and Untamed:*
A Field Guide for the Vagabond Believer,
Chapter 8—The Jump

S&U Experience 2—The Album

"Where Once I Feared to Walk" is a song about walking with God. When we walk with God, we find ourselves not only dreaming but also chasing down those dreams. And even when it seems that we have failed in our pursuit, if we stay close to God, we will see that our feet tread where once we feared to walk.

www.surrenderedanduntamed.com/fearedtowalk

Where Once I Feared to Walk

We went walking out in the field
Yeah, late tonight
Could see our breath each dream exhaled
beneath the half moon light

This is Life, You said to me
This declared round Your pipe
This is where it all works out
In dreaming we're alive

I have dreamed and still believe
I have risked and I have lost
But looking down I see my feet
where once I feared to walk

So we go walking out in this field
to claim our destiny
And if by chance it seems we've failed
then here's to bigger dreams.

S&U Experience 3—The Film

We ended the DVD with Alex and Sibu arriving safely at the South Pole. It was a magical moment that was made more so because of what they overcame to get there. But to be honest, when I (Joel) watched the footage of their joyful arrival, I was initially a little unimpressed. I had seen Alex's footage and photos from the top of Everest and multiple other mountains. The South Pole looked . . . well, exactly like the spot they had started from. Sure there is a massive United States science base located at the pole, but everything about the landscape is almost identical. There is nothing at the pole, except a sign and a pole, to tell you that you have arrived somewhere significant.

This fact didn't go unnoticed by Alex and Sibu. Initially they arrived with an excitement that, as Mark puts it, "led to overwhelming and spontaneous shouts of praise," yet over a relatively short period of time they went back to exactly what they had been doing for the previous 65 days. They set up their tent, they cooked their food, and they sat in the cold. Even though not much changed regarding routine, both Alex and Sibu will be the first to say, of all their expeditions, in many ways, this was the most meaningful.

No matter how big the promises of God may be in our lives, the beauty and wonder of a surrendered and untamed life is found in the midst of the journey as much as it is found in the fulfillment of a particular promise.

Below is a link to what happened after their triumphant arrival as well as the revelation of what they took away from this insane journey.

www.surrenderedanduntamed.com/notrace

The Beginning . . .

Thanks for taking this journey with us. We encourage you to revisit this guide over the coming days and weeks; especially the meditations where you defined your promises from God. We also think it might be a good idea if you were to wash your hands after using the restroom. It has nothing to do with this guide, but it's probably not a bad habit to form.

We challenge you to set goals. Nothing is accomplished with just a vision. You need both the vision—your promise—and then real, practical mile markers. There is an art to setting goals. You have to dream big *and* plan attainable steps. It's the marriage of the magical and practical.

On this journey, God will continue to reveal His heart for you. He will continue to give you a clear vision regarding your promise. So dream, and then begin to take the steps.

God bless your journey!

Mark Batterson serves as lead pastor of National Community Church (www.theaterchurch.com) in Washington, DC. NCC was recognized as one of the Most Innovative and Most Influential Churches in America by *Outreach Magazine* in 2008. One church with nine services in five locations, NCC is focused on reaching emerging generations. Approximately 70 percent of NCCers are single twentysomethings.

The vision of NCC is to meet in movie theaters at metro stops throughout the DC area. NCC also owns and operates the largest coffeehouse on Capitol Hill. In 2008, Ebenezers was recognized as the #1 coffeehouse in the metro DC area by *AOL CityGuide*.

Mark has two master's degrees from Trinity Evangelical Divinity School in Chicago, Illinois. He is the author of the bestselling books *In a Pit with a Lion on a Snowy Day* and *Wild Goose Chase*. His latest release is *Primal*. And he is a daily blogger at www.mark batterson.com.

Mark is married to Lora and they live on Capitol Hill with their three children, Parker, Summer, and Josiah.

Jason Clark is codirector of the Surrendered & Untamed series. He is the author of *Surrendered and Untamed: A Field Guide for the Vagabond Believer* and a published writer with Thomas Nelson for Donald Miller's *The Open Table: An Invitation to Walk with God*. Jason is also a writer for several projects with Switchvert Multimedia that span commercials and documentaries to sitcom TV programs and film.

A graduate of Elim Bible Institute (1995), Jason has held three worship leadership positions since 1996. He is a recording artist and has released three albums. The first two, *For the Vagabond Believer* and *Sacrifice,* were recorded with his band of seven years, Fringe. His most recent album is entitled *Surrendered & Untamed.* Much of the music from that album is used on the S&U DVDs.

He is a speaker and worship leader at churches, conferences, and retreats across the country. Jason and his wife, Karen, live in Cornelius, North Carolina, with their three children, Madeleine True, Ethan Wilde, and Eva Blaze.

Joel Clark is the codirector of Surrendered & Untamed as well as the president of Switchvert, a production house based out of South Africa and Washington, DC. Joel has been Switchvert's writer and director since its conception in 2003. Besides creating the Surrendered and Untamed project, Joel has filmed and coauthored an evangelistic/discipleship DVD/book series titled *The Open Table* with Don Miller (author of the bestselling book *Blue Like Jazz*). Joel is also author of the forthcoming *Do It for the Story.* He has shot numerous films and documentaries around the world on issues ranging from child slavery in Haiti to kidnapping in Nigeria, and HIV/AIDS in sub-Saharan Africa. He has also conceived and created every production on his company's website, www.switchvert.com.

Joel is married to the love of his life, Megan, and they live together in Washington, DC.

Permissions

Page 24

"My Beautiful Song" © 2006 Jason Clark. Used by permission. All rights reserved.

Page 37

"When the Stars Fall Like Rain" © 2006 Jason Clark. Used by permission. All rights reserved.

Page 53

"Only Dead Men Can Go" © 2006 Jason Clark. Used by permission. All rights reserved.

Page 68

"Where Once I Feared to Walk" © 2006 Jason Clark. Used by permission. All rights reserved.

Stunning Cinematography
and Powerful True Stories Help You Discover
a Meaningful and Adventurous Faith

Whether experienced in a group setting or individually, the combined impact of the book, the DVD, and this participant's guide will ignite your faith and stir your imagination as it leads you on a journey to the edges of the earth—and the depths of your faith.

BakerBooks
a division of Baker Publishing Group
www.BakerBooks.com

Available Wherever Books Are Sold

Visit
www.**surrendered**and**untamed**.com
for regularly updated content,
including:

- Excerpts from Alex Harris's video diary

- Video blogs from Mark Batterson,
  Jason Clark, and Alex Harris

- Interactive conversations on faith
  and adventure

- And much more!

Many of the song lyrics featured in the book
Surrendered and Untamed are from
Jason Clark's latest album.

This album *Surrendered+Untamed* by Clark
is available on **iTunes** and **Amazon**.

Or check it out at
www.surrenderedanduntamed.com

REVIEWS FOR THE ALBUM *SURRENDERED+UNTAMED* BY CLARK

"It only gets better from there, each track epic in theme and grandeur. Both lyrically and instrumentally, the album is wildly creative and builds an atmosphere of awe that lends itself to sincere worship . . . [This album] will lead you as far into the presence of God as you are willing to go. You can't ask for more than that."

—**Kevan Breitinger**, about.com guest reviewer

"What shines the most on this album is the songwriting. These are great songs; they are songs that mean something. They search, they hope, they fear, they beg for change. This album is simply astounding, don't miss out on it."

—**Mark Fisher**, infuse.cgi.org